FREE VERSE EDITIONS

Edited by Jon Thompson

PUPPET WARDROBE

Books by Daniel Tiffany

Radio Corpse: Imagism and the Cryptaesthetic of Ezra Pound (1995)
Toy Medium: Materialism and Modern Lyric (2000)

PUPPET WARDROBE

Daniel Tiffany

Parlor Press
West Lafayette, Indiana
www.parlorpress.com

Parlor Press LLC, West Lafayette, Indiana 47906

Printed in the United States of America
S A N: 2 5 4 - 8 8 7 9

Library of Congress Cataloging-in-Publication Data

Tiffany, Daniel Newton
  Puppet wardrobe / Daniel Tiffany.
    p. cm. -- (Free verse editions)
  ISBN 1-932559-93-0 (pbk. : acid-free paper) -- ISBN 1-932559-
94-9 (hardcover : acid-free paper) -- ISBN 1-932559-95-7 (adobe
ebook)
  I. Title.
  PS3570.I335P87 2006
  811'.6--dc22
                                        2006029643

Printed on acid-free paper.

Cover design by Amy Dakos

Cover illustration from *The Visible Compendium*, a film by Lawrence
  Jordan. Used by permission.

Parlor Press, LLC is an independent publisher of scholarly and
trade titles in print and multimedia formats. This book is available in
print and Adobe eBook formats from Parlor Press on the Internet
at http://www.parlorpress.com. For submission information or to
find out about Parlor Press publications, write to Parlor Press, 816
Robinson St., West Lafayette, Indiana, 47906, or e-mail editor@
parlorpress.com.

For my father

(1925–1988)

Contents

Acknowledgments

Grateful acknowledgment is made to editors of the following magazines, where poems from *Puppet Wardrobe* first appeared, sometimes with other titles and, in some cases, with differences in the text:

American Literary Review
Boston Review
Colorado Review
Denver Quarterly
LIT
New American Writing
New Review of Literature
Paris Review
Passages North
Pequod
Perihelion
Poetrydaily.org
Quarterly West
The Germ
Tin House
VOLT

PUPPET WARDROBE

Si spie, si no spie,
foist, nip, shave, and spare not.

Anon. canting lyric

ARCADE MODEL

MASTER'S GONE AWAY

Supposing a doll of mysterious origin,
a mechanical marvel, falls into your hands.
And suppose the doll, restored to life, signs the name
—the very signature—of the chemist who made it,
long dead. And now recall the print pulled in 1793
showing the toy, a girl today, richly dressed as a boy.

Suppose all that—for the doll *is* a writing machine—
and suppose it held in its periodic mind,
long before it went astray in the world,
a cartoon of the ship that would take it abroad
and a sketch of its maker—some say—or a self-portrait,
a study of Eros in chariot pulled by a butterfly.

And now suppose it scrawls—for a penny—these words
for you, announcing its return as a god:
Without eyes I see, without tongue I speak.

The Names of the Dice

A bale of barred cinque-deuces.
A bale of flat sice-aces.
A bale of barred cater-treys.
A bale of flat cater-treys.
A bale of fullams of the best making.
A bale of light greviers.
A bale of langrets contrary to the vantage.
A bale of gourds with as many high men as low men, for passage.
A bale of demies.
A bale of long dice for even and odd.
A bale of bristles.
A bale of direct contraries.

Nothing But Bonfires

Before night steals from your side
someone will hear the news.
Nothing but bonfires
and the unborn
flicker in the oracle's face,
eyes laboring
under a bushel—and you,
an audience of dummies in the dark.

The mole tells,
wringing word of the chasm
from an acorn of sleep:
on it goes, on and on,
harvesting vernix and fugitive colors,
the errand of the eye
boiling in a ditch—and you,
pink string and sealing wax.

8

Sappho's Tantrum

The morning flew by.
Not that it matters, it's nothing
like flying, or finding a dime behind a cushion,
merganser-filled and vaguely Russian,

still in this world
but out of its mind
—my mind, that is—the only mind it has
to lose. None but the item going fast.

And why are there none? None
to explain what we see. It remains to be seen.
It can't be "seeing" falling brightly away,
like a snowfall.

It's too rouge, the ratio unto death,
to lure the drones—a dizzy chain of bees—
to drown themselves with any luck
in one of Sappho's tantrums on the page.

EXPLOSIVELY CHEAP

Over the rotten scarlet & yellow moss
a great parade against all
knowledge drew
near. You there, what for stand you
there, she asked. Spying
the weather
I claimed as I checked the driveway to see
if any strange cars had pulled up
outside my house.
I conquered the old notion of kidnappers
and child-stealers being
a common trade.
And other names for claptraps
to ease the pocket
of its burden.
In my last I saw so much misty shuffling
that I took them all by chance
as I sailed—
a century of wisdom in every purse,
a cheery *aloha!* in each
and every clip.
The silkie's golden trucks bear down
like flame, her whole life
a first
of April. The statue curls its finger—
she starts your tongue
on tiptoe.
Her pockets are crammed with it.

Ham Hound Crave

Powdery timbers
jutting from beds of marl
and trash, columns
blurred to brackish lines
diced in a foot of water.
Greetings, old business,

ham hound crave:
our guide strolled back
barefoot into the haze of the ruined arena.
He drew a map in the dirt.
Heard something, say a woman and a dollar.
Ain't said a mumbling word.

The drone of a lumber scow
rose from the estuary:
the listless, the lollers
stirred in the shade,
each face a bead in a blackberry's comb,
glazed, glowing like a wick.

WEREWOLF IN SELVAGE

Once, when you showed up for work
after blazing all night
someone said the trigger word
by mistake and you turned over
the things you'd stolen. Just like that.

Once, as you straightened your mask
at the Oscar bash, your friends plotted
to have you put away.

Once, when you had disappeared into the woods,
you leaned over the wash basin
to have a word with me.

And when you turned back
again the roads buckled
because there was no more room in the fields,
oh loved one in the great fiery mood,
the not-asking mood.

Nightspot

You'll like my big-girl outfit—
just make sure you get the signals
right: once the collar's set
and the cuffs, nod once to put ice in

my veins, twice and your kisses turn
to riddles—say who I am—to favors
punished, struck from the books.
Under vows to make infraction sing.

Then harness me—for breaking—
and whisper to the docile dray
in heavy guise: uproot me here.
Pass quickly on the stairs

a girl undressing—you—
now hasten to the idol.
Do not take another step.
You're free to go, if you wish

—it's best at twilight—
or wait to be questioned.
I see it in the air,
permission somehow stolen,

I don't understand who's there
in my place, a star like a blueprint
spreading from nail to calf,
an image of the engine. Say who I am.

Seaside

Cupped to my mouth
in the thick of reason's
unreason, a hand bottles
up a little cry.
More, more, it cracks
to no one, sir.
Thumbish its work, and birdlike,
though I plead a syllable more:
crumb and wick,
brackish I like
and briny waters too.
Much at the fold
my tongue is taught.
Untry, untouch the naked oyster,
all throat and folded foot,
bound twelve ways
to spoon the fool.

SHINY FOLK

The wind goes on troubling the youngest
at 2 AM standing meeting in the dwelling

house. Begun with step manner two songs.
Then marched two or three songs. Then labored

in our rooms. Broke bands, had many simple
gifts and a good meeting. No inspiration.

The lights cut out and we can see you,
the world's people, from a distance. Remember

the young Brethren & Sisters need to learn
to be simple for themselves & gain that mortification

which they need, in order to be able to help
others, as this work is calculated to help them

as well as the uncultivated spirits. In the evening
we have standing meeting & admit the Spirits

of different Nations; a very singular and strange
meeting. The natives pressed in upon us & begged

a bit of privilege, we sung two or three
of their songs, leaped, hooted & rejoiced

with them. They told how much they had learned
there & how the shiny folk took them in.

Cataract

Starlet, green hackle and bone of the lure,
a toy, not more than a snowflake,
vanishing into my sleeve.
Looked on the ground

found a little jaw bone
losing sleep, how it
rears from the body a child,
from the raft of its bed

accusing whoever sails with the child
—grand mal—a voice marooned,
repeating parts of a song
it cannot master.

And by serving it goes unseen,
unknown—even the books
it makes are dolls—and some recite charms
to make the air the cataract and the dew confess.

Honey in the Lion's Ear

What death wants,
that too, forgetting much in tea's desire,
in friendship hiding sorrow,
tattles under morphine,
farming the lunatic
and the light between.

What Death wants
—without guessing again—
survives the surly dawn
bearded with lace:
a thing in the limelight
the neighboring clock tells me.

You unmuzzled is too.
Mocked by flowers
and one last snag:
strange rescue, real lilacs
sewn to my body.
The dead wake over the hull.

Not now, but *now,*
a visitor finds you
pulling your nightshirt
through a pair of hands
like a frightened magician:
oh what was it was your father after?

What Death wants
I learned from holding you
the night your hands
a gardener's hands
began to fill with water.
I learned its secret quickly.

And it—*shh*—good-natured cheat,
it spreads over the living body,
the mouth first, its native color,
those arms I always wanted,
hard as hickory.
You tasted love with half a mind.

Hybrid of petal and hoof,
black anger
every word now swallows,
tickle and burn. A corpse prefers
romantic weather.
Cassandra speaks and no one listens.

Winter rocket, fiddle dock,
succumbs to itself in flight.
One of you holds my breath:
the engine chokes and rattles, it
stalls in thirty thousand feet of air,
unawakened, sovereign.

What Death wants
it yields: a meteor, a silhouette,
the style of immortality.
Oh, there's more to know
or more to come.
And it will have your eyes.

What Death wants
a treble dark confides:
a puzzle in the trade,
not prey but icons
speaking to a fool
through the candle hedge.

HORN LAKE ROAD

Then you have burned
your hat for nothing
and carried the mountain-top
stick in vain.

Colonel Mustard
with the candlestick in the cab.
Dolls dose for a trick,
set to mauling in domelight.

Nice. You find your way
to the empty house of some big producer
roused in anger from his sleep
by two strangers who put him back
to sleep with a knock on the head
and carry him off into the night.

DARKNESS COUNTS

Wrist to wrist,
pilot light to blood,
turning nether nether by the look
of it: here comes ancient nothingness.
Ankles shackled here comes to,
here comes everyone.
On the early side.
Whose body still away
sleepless it wears,
a night like any other.
White quiver,
see-through dead man
rues the day him put
in stocks to blush.
Lovely boy, you say.
Darkness counts for something.
Making up,
darkness counts.

SKIN-SKIN-SKIN

Shepherd's fire, unattended, on the plain.
Parings rise through tallow and ash.
Shoulder, thigh, shower glass.
Strapping, tender as a prawn,
its nowhere curls
along the nowhere seam.
Ocotillo. Ocotillo Wells.

With rain, first bristle, then bone,
the shallow sand cannot keep you.
Beard gathering simples in a ditch.
Towels stacked on marble,
untouched in milky light.
Something passiver shines
on Teddy Bear spines, red foil of a kiss.

COME AND SEE

No bigger than cocktail lamps, some trees
dying of curiosity. White cedar, relic forest
pinned to a bluff—the mere thought
chiselled to life. Stone torch, auspicious
archive of the weather of late:
rainfall patterns Mozart's day,
a dry spell for the witch trials in Salem.

The water never shows its face,
but what does it matter: come,
come and see.
Roofbeam thick the peat in June
and my child is light enough
to walk, where we would sink,
to the islands.

Orchards find me in the silvery dark.
Pale skiff returning to dust
in the tall shore grass,
take me to rest in your bedding bluff,
ocher and oarlock,
my lamp, my ore,
take me below.

MR. SO AND SO

Summer's dusty heart
points like a phonograph arm
to the waxy gear in the frost,

the tin scoop on the maple,
the sugar gear.
Oh, he's here somewhere,

the leaves say so,
and every limb, every blade,
glitters in the woven shade.

The children cannot come to table
just now. The rose is out of town.
A secret summit robs the air.

The rare dwarf iris shivers at dusk,
lake iris, emperor's delight,
sparkling in a bog between two bays,

like Ovid in exile on the Black Sea,
had he chosen to live
so far from Rome.

Spy & Beauty Treatment

Needle threadless, gameboy of the fair confession
—it must have been here I lost my way—
as they often leave the oaks half cut down
till the barkmen come to pill them.

Sideways I looked for hope and fear.
Magic perpendiculars. Chin deep,
the country chin deep in rumors of flight.
Cold-frames, breezeways, storm doors.

Slang for the pink redoubt. For
I had imagined Oundle after lime burnt
at the kiln. Orison. Knife-and-shearlessness.
Oundle were a place of other days.

Mazed, them busk and boon, my box
of lucifers. Everything and its opposite.
A pounding harder than nature
could bear. Wets unpretending beauties.

All under leaves, the leaves of life,
triple glazing protection for white folk.
Last copy changing hands. Sews nicely.
And the swinkt hedger at his supper sat.

An old white thorn full of fame,
the ox man fleured. So there.
Swallow of poppy seeds,
tint of delight.

Off the hooks, waiting to be repaired
till repairs are useless. Plowman purple
with cold, so crowded with awes that bye and bye
the fields will be dressed with nothing.

HARD NICKNAMEY SYSTEM

Heist

Girls wear nightclothes and sometimes sleep
in liquid form, en route. Black baby grand.
Tart, blue-blind, plum-like fruit of the sloe,
she missed her second fitting. Were it not so.

Beuys calls from Hamburg. Evening. Light dying.
Though she may wander from her own kind.
Speculation leaked to rival. Car waiting.
Key where she said it was, as per flame job.

Swiss plates & papers missing—fuckwad—two days
to go, car trapped inside Germany. Prophetic dream
according to the place. Back under *Mistress A.*

The thief must know me. Descend on Baltic port
for mezzotint. Some trick to it. Try giving
it away on the streets. Must make night ferry.

RED *VELOCE*

No tugboat squeeze, no greasy greasy tug
this, niche, faint from shelling sea. Pop duchess,
rock-ribbed in jeweller's belt, out late
with him, who drove it off the pier—a guess.

Fan-shaped grill, icon nosing two feet
merely, dreamy, under sickened waters. Why
Monica Vitti counter-clockwise in the street?
Why. None to see the crane—cat's cradle,

sore midnight—fetch the Alfa from the drink.
So that we may forget none of what drowning
Neptune drowns, no cubic feet of undersea
in lingerie, dark as a pupil: Giulietta streaming

under ether in a sling. Horn aglitter.
Not unlike the rig, all stirrup and cuff,
feeding cherub to flame, indigo-veined & nicer
than nice. At the whim of the dancers below.

STOLEN FURS

1

Long heat of the rope's decay:
kid man on the kid, summer
peering through the mossy vent.
No one knows her real name,
who stirs in its sleep,
the hills' sleeve caught in the wind.

2

Reflection in a barber's window:
a pretty vandal thrice
her age in bootless air.
Child bride
in robing-rooms of nonesuch,
pulled like a dove from a hat.

3

Reflex summons her mouth
folded in its legs, rose stack
of firewood burnt by wind—its embrace,
faint rhombs of shade.
Ox from dawn,
the dreamer's hips nod.

4

The net gorged with harm is enough,
enough. A moth eats through the shroud
of May. Kings breed in the mire.
Leisure, cold as the element
a fish swims in. Evening spills
a cache of tools.

5

Cape Cod and a pack of Salems, too,
a phrase—uh-huh—Billie drags for you:
no musing decked or spoonful
measured but noon,
noon doll thrown through kin—
a prowler knocking the bijoux bin.

6

Catch and bait
bobbing in the gutter of a miracle,
bone coiled in a ball of sleep:
frantic the vandal
branching after
anything in its way.

OFF

Let it not be said
and the breeders rolled up the map
showing all the turquoise mines in Arizona,
evanished figures and landscape, live,
the quasi-credent, eve-lengthened bud. . . . Islet
of ether in a whole Sky of blackest Cloudage.

Something came over them,
nay, the swan of objectation,
if that's the word she used.
Cell floor decorated with torn strips,
weather fit for man nor beast.
It lived eleven days.

Of course, any child's a picture of something
far away (and something close)
gone twice to seed,
but this one's good for plenty more:
it took the mold of a wish
come true—the kind that spells an end

to this or that, before its time.
A glimpse of something hideous
from her window the morning
she conceived. And, oh—
the policeman's grin,
they both remember that.

CAVE OF THE GOLDEN CALF

Leave a little on your plate,
as never you are told to do,
a thing-in-itself, replete,

for ghosts to swipe, who
mire, who furnish proof.
Fairest one, to one of two

camps confined. Woof-woof.
Spun-sugar tits. Libraries lost,
girls gone missing. Poof!

A novice writhes on the post.
Of wrens (a mouth begins to water)
the room holds one, at most.

The crowd goes under,
a child with a toy in tow.
Nobody's business—leave her

be, someone says. For now.
Fired up, each takes a turn,
breath-on-mirror. And how.

MILK MUSTACHE

A girl—fourteen?—sniffing
Georgie-Porgie's round-the-clock burn
backs into a clearing—
any old place will do.
Everything's wet already

after a week of cold rain,
a woodsy spot missing a wall
or two, each of us answering
nature's call, though my stroke's
a little fishy, my luck spectacular.

She rips—oh no, princess—the daintiest
of habits, a mere pocketsquare
to fuss with, but swoons again
with a glance at her scent
in the darkness of the lived moment.

I try to make her hands more private,
more *hers*. Nothing doing.
Caught in the dwarf light,
the very tombstone
of her careless debut.

Hadn't a Had My Pistol

My second thoughts blushed over them
and I
burnt them for a long while.

Spreading him but served
to cry
the riddle of my used-to-be.

With a linkie down and a day
like rain
the trickling down did feel.

No dainties will you lack,
dirt bag,
and I will pay the shot.

Even my itches have itches.
Boo hoo.
And drumlie grew his ee.

He hazard his make shift
for learning
as heedless as he please.

If you need a red crayola why
you don't
just use the top of my head.

Doubtless there cropped him a white
water-lily
and won a song for its pains.

I take the barrettes and leave the fuzz balls
passing
shepherds & feast goers in the night.

And in the want of sealing
wax
seald it with pitch.

I'm afraid if I start
I'll never stop—
a small book of Arithmetic, heavenly footman.

It seemed to stand out of the worlds
eye yet
there was occasional droppers in.

A little beside the ash
he nimbling
darkish cotton flowerd gown.

Next, they find his code
his number,
the worlds roam. Late them beg through life.

Steeple to the middle Third wild,
half
the clock under trumpet vines.

The reading world has forgot him
as the wild
bees honey is forgotten in the meadow grass.

I can smell it from here.
What's-his-name,
what time he picking you up?

FLASH, ETC

Way back in the back
he found the last bit of human cargo:
tin-lipped and pale as the living dust
on a moth's wing,
a busted zenith, god
all over the floor.

SUGAR GEAR

Is it possible
that sullen freak for dice is
wearing stripes, the devil's cloth, ruse cut,
so late in bone adventure?

John Doe enriped,
is it—Pla Ce Bo—and she be sib,
nineteen again & wonderly between.
Impossible.

Bombed on Neccos,
only riot could decide what tenders
with him fray, mischieve, gold of tissue,
half surmise.

After all
a terrible storm towards evening
tipped over and so on. I remember it well.
Is it possible?

The less said.
89 etchings of frog in the road,
Walloon, Buckwheat—who is this, who?
The hunter in sight.

And what if a mirror
stops like a clock? Krazy Kat on silver
nitrate, bought dear and ought,
is it not?

Downtown Science

What cheerful country smolders in your gaze?
A pigeon's muddy dream, a peddler's chant.
Siren says, wax and bait and go aslant,
who cures the hen of the moth with *tarte anglaise*.

A grid of little favors breaks your fall
to Earth, to endless rut and violence,
but if the air's a shallow grave, your skull
will tear the rotting nap of eloquence:
a Fabergé egg and I the fool
to wind the stem, the crank of innocence.

VIRTUOSO

Then you'll have real trouble on your hands.
Every thought magnified and still no sign
of the amateur proving the scant Middle Ring
to be one of the "curves of volition"
—a winding balustrade—in the Chanel Pavilion
for Nazi brass and geisha, or if the iron

finial tipping the balustrade—a pomegranate—
turns out to be dust, through and through,
a relic of the dubious Inner Ring. Have in
then Sergeant Ferrier, my horse behind is bare!
Absence abasheth me, warm to the touch,
absence is my foe, and here comes Goofy now,

all but human, signing autographs on napkins
for the kids and making them laugh.

Lux Aeterna

Standard model.
Brutal model.
Fishnet model.
Private model.
Model for you.
Chafed model.
Plus model.
Arcade model.
Blacklist model.
Nebuchadnezzar model.
Egg-and-dart model.
Breach model.

CAPTAIN, CAPTAIN

Reared by hand
the cade-lamb
rakes her trick.

Black seed shining,
hurricane pie,
I-don't-want-no-junk.

Carve up naughty,
Captain, captain,
Slip me in the dozens.

It makes me sick, it makes me well—
Last night I walked
And all last night before.

Grass caught in willow
there is none.
Agave, none. Agave.

Bells known to the cade-lamb
reared by hand,
whispering, everlasting.

Carve up naughty,
Captain, captain,
Slip me in the dozens.

It makes me sick, it makes me well—
Last night I walked
And all last night before.

Tract Containing the
Sudden Death of the Liar

You learned to love ideas
as a boy in a rowboat—so the story goes—
spared by the guards
for the relic of your blood
—okay, whatever—and the old tune
you sang at dusk,
though now you will not sing
and I have come to this marsh
where you told me to wait,
not waiting, but crowding
the unappointed hour.

The cold sun made me
drowsy, discipled—was it then
you swam from the dark
like a sea dragon
losing everything
at the baccarat table?

There, there,
little monster,
all eyes on the floor
of the Roman mosaic.

Let's see, how does it go, again?

Inverted and drenched
in the dome of the yellow garage,
you show me the way down.
You hold the door for me.

My fear of the angel
dials the sun backwards—too late,
you've gone missing already.
Off eating Pharaoh in the tall grass.

Light sprays from the gills
you open behind his ears,
light dialing into bungalows
behind the dusty motor court.

QUARRY

On the road to the village
we hear footsteps
quickening out of the dark.
A solitary figure runs by us
without a sound,
hands lifted about its head.

You say it is a young girl
and I an old man.
The moon will not rise till dawn.

The exact words lie
in close flowery hiding:
shadow, leash, grate—
excavation and prey,
ebb of confinement
astray on a moonless night.

GIMLET EYES

If you want an audience, we could
park under a streetlight and zip down
the windows before you open your blouse.
The Chinese are full of superstitions.

We might as well be sailors drowned at sea,
the dash so cold the dials tick like embers
in the dark. Your face darts through the wheel
like a fish—a mob—to put its mouth to me.

Someone walking by would see your curls
bobbing in the well. Let's give the world a peek.
You smuggled me into Shanghai once:
now tell, oh tell, how you did murder me.

SEE NO BODY SAW

Too young for a steed or the odd gazelle,
I married the bench of a swan's chariot

and held my breath: the trees were fuming
bales of camphor, a recipe purling from hides

of animals after a storm, after a spell.
The old calliope raced ahead of the lumbering toy

until the lights caught up in a blur
and the whole room went under,

submerged at the whim of a puppet
I'd seen at the fair—or had it spied me?—

coming to life with a card in its hand.
I turned to wave to someone thinking

the hooves never touch the floor. And when
it turned its head, the eyes of the violet Bay

blazed to the size of plums and swept
its lacquered mane behind a wave,

exploding from the iris of its grave.
But when I dropped my hands to look again,

its eyes were quiet and streaked with light,
like marbles cracked in a fleeting mask,

the eyes of a god shipwrecked
in a mare's head of human thought.

Skirt Metamorphoses

Extinct, no.
Never stops fingering
its iris its small
vocabulary, the forge smolders
in the tides of the trick top note of limes.
Because of you know who.

The gods can abdicate,
the way they were.
Violet crumble, wicked chair,
the wherewithal
of air. In crucible her scent,
sweet gum from shiver
and hiss of iron
doused in a bath of stars.

Onto something.
In one darkness demise writing.
Parting insensibly
the matchbox
teepees and ponies
scattered on the hearth.

Verdigris scale, why not,
the ground disturbed,
if that's how you say it,
retail frost and such.
Green wood hell yes for all
but one of its tines.

Good enough to bury itself
before it dawns
on her.

Hard Nicknamey System

Lazy bed—green the fits of L & D
from the Candle going out in the socket.
Then and only then
coldness perhaps & paralysis
in all tangible ideas.

So it grew paler in tint—and now,
where is it?
She urges him to be more explicit.
He tells a hundred lies
all flowr-gem'd with Honeysuckles.

Blame the sea—unquiet element
made only for wonder and use.
Sailors are very often angry. Forget
the beautiful girl bathing in a half mask.
Something gone wrong with the silence.

Drunk with a black-hued scarlet
in one, bees & a mousetrap. In another
a lovers chain, of its own
wildly peopled with small ashes—& in the same
recess a ditcher's cap hung to dry.

Objects, namely, Fire, handle, Comb
at first Look
shine apparently on the green tips
opposite the parlor, but in a few seconds
they acquire ideal Distance.

And a mill of good snishing to pry.
Sleepo. I thought it was lipliner—duh,
it's eyeliner! I mean it's
not like I'm asking you
to get him over here or anything.

He frit the lark up raking—whoa!
And blue-cheeked Dowbie there will be
with thumbless Katie's beau,
who gade to the south for manners quick,
who gade to the south for manners.

With pretty baby-wreaths of smoke.
With her & no one with us
all as cold
and calm as a deep Frost.
Nape, one-berry, ox-eye.

Just the tick tock and the trail to go by.
Enough to give shadow
for my face & just at the foot
one tall foxglove—there I lay and slept.
It was so very soft.

On French green paper
the road is lined with lamps.
Skeletons fall to dust in the air
—that's what I'm trying to tell you—
my rider's gone on Horn Lake Road.

SHIVAREE

THE BRANDS OF CUPID

Lord Byron: Moon, owl a ventriloquist—
what should we think?

Tragic Mulatto: White dialogues de mundo.

Lord Byron: Is this the way
he takes to insult me?

Vague Adam: Dreamed lucky and
woke up cold in.

20471120:   Detox time!

Tragic Mulatto: We pin back the hair falling in his eyes.

Westwest: She kneels down and paints one of his nails.

20471120:   *Femme Slab,* the label says.

Westwest: He starts to lick his nails
so she holds onto his head.

20471120:   Jelly hind groom.

Lord Byron: I wrote or rather thought
poems made Botanical arrangements.

Westwest: Would you care to order something from our
liquid list?

Lord Byron:	The head of Female Veto [the Queen] separated from her fucking head.
Vague Adam:	Now that's what I call a treat.
Tragic Mulatto:	Ah, that pink stranger we call dust.
20471120:	A close shave.
Westwest:	Anything is possible.
Vague Adam:	The printing of mutilated Editions so beautiful as gradually to produce utter oblivion of the entire ones.
20471120:	Pretend-drinking. I hate it.
The Lord's Animals:	We pretend to drink, we pretend to choke, we fall down.
Westwest:	Enough, enough.
Lord Byron:	How can I ever thank you?
Westwest:	In white garments beautifully disordered. . . .
20471120:	A chorus of Rational Recreations.

NAMELESS BROKEN DANDY

The phone rings.

Flower-de-Luce: My real nails don't fall off.

Upset Kitty: He's taken out his little penknife
and twinn'd the sweet babe.

20471120: His master's voice.

Upset Kitty: KGB. I miss it something terrible.

Old Sultan: Coals made pretty—wood kill'd by fire.

Lord Byron: A bird shop at the corner of Wood Street?

Tragic Mulatto: Sometimes I don't know why.

Flower-de-Luce: Pretending to be mermaids

Upset Kitty: Either way, I lose.

Plank o wude: He doesn't have a nice bone in his body.

Old Sultan: He saild with him but doubtless
child Harrold had no existence
with the world then.

Flower-de-Luce: Hint to gentleman of one Shirty:
laundry at fire.

LORD BYRON'S FUNERAL

20471120:	Time makes strange work with early fancys.

Old Sultan: I see Saturn at the end of town,
ten thousand mourners at a glance.

Flower-de-Luce: Almost 1/20 of the whole Heaven
in appearance—green with huge scars
of bare blue stone dust—and beyond
a flight of steps
leading to the temple.

Westwest: Solitary persons are siding up the hedges.

Old Sultan: I wonder if he'll come back with an accent.

Westwest: The young girl standing by me
counted the carriages in her mind
as they passed & she told me
there was 63 or 64 in all.

20471120: And the gilt ones that lead the procession are empty.

Flower-de-Luce: I knew it could not be a common one
by the curiosity keeping watch
on every face.

Old Sultan: A fine collection of uncles.

20471120: Emphasized and gone.

Flower-de-Luce: A book on bees and a restless
desire for glass hives.

Westwest: Strange navigation.

INTERLUDE: SEVEN TEARS

LB: Down among the hongerey worms I sleep.
FDL: So well paid see you be.
LB: Sans peer.
FDL: Hurt-sickle, rib grass.
LB: Naked shelving crags.
FDL: Wha?
LB: Injun' out of kitchen came.
FDL: Girt gravel—& green gravel.
LB: If it comes to that.
FDL: The bouche of Court.
LB: Stones burnt.
FDL: Nothing showy is liked of.
LB: On my left, my left.
FDL: In distempered dream.
LB: Go-to-bed-at-noon.
FDL: And cast I never know what.
LB: The versing box.
FDL: Discovered very late.
LB :   Straight with him in fambling cheats.
FDL: A dimple in the tomb.

VAGABONDIA

Many of his names are now afloat in the city.

By autopsy we get
a certain knowledge of things.

And the top stones of all the bridges
we pass are busy with two-letter names
rudely cut with a knife.

Undoubted marks of autoptic faith.

Odd young man on board
lame of one foot
on which he wore a cloth shoe.

Not to mention his autopsy
of a fine lady's poem.

Small hail from the sky did fall.

The autopsy shows . . .

Fond of bathing in the sea & going ashore
to see ruins in a rough sea
when it required 6 hands to manage the boat.

The autopsy shows the ball to be nowhere.

The infamous promiscuity of things.

Reverend Gadget

Westwest:	And pieces of naked water make me cholo to look over it.
Tragic Mulatto:	Gude red gowd it was his hire.
Flower-de-Luce:	A Brusher up of Convulsia & Tetanus upon the innocent Canvas.
2047110:	Uncommonly cold in his feelings of animal love.
Plank o wude:	Do I smell cake?
Old Sultan:	He never travelled but in a map.
Flower-de-Luce:	Fancy it a stain.
Tragic Mulatto:	Scum—viz—the monarchical part, the poet's eye in its tipsy hour.
Westwest:	Until he borrow you with kisses.

Thank You, Vertigo

Tragic Mulatto: The colors that show best
by candlelight are White
Carnation and a kinde of Sea-Water Green.

Westwest: Little hells of color,
hence she becomes the willing
slave of the Eyes & Ears of others.

Flower-de-Luce: How dare she!

Plank o wude: Ale-Hoof, Candy Tuft, Sauce Alone.

Lord Byron: Consult the Bee Maidens.

Old Sultan: Blow Book.

Westwest: It runs in his veins.

Tragic Mulatto: Whatsoever bloweth on it
will give the picture
of whatsoever he is
naturally addicted unto.

Plank o wude: That has a nice ring to it.

LAVENDER THRIFT

Flower-de-Luce: How quiet it is tonight.

20471120: Item—murmur of a stream—Item—well with shadows—
Item—a day of clouds & threatening Showrlets.

Tragic Mulatto: I took him for a swan.

Westwest: I noticed the cracking of the stubs.

Upset Kitty: Always beheading his dolls.

Tragic Mulatto: Stalls of toys & sweet horses on wheels
with their flowing manes and lambs
their red necklaces & box cuckoos.

Westwest: I can feel myself blush.

Tragic Mulatto: I take a tiny taste of each thing.

Flower-de-Luce: Running unconsciously on errands
for Pigeons milk, glass-eyed needles . . .

Childe scolding
a flower: The wet wets a' my yellow hair.

Westwest: She turned her back upon the room
her face upon the wa.

The Lord's
Animals: In the brave nights so early.

Old Sultan: I have often lingerd a minute on the stile
                 to hear the wood pigeons clapping their wings
                 among the dark oaks.

Plank o wude: Till I got out of my knowledge
                 when the very wild flowers
                 and birds seemed to forget me.

O Per Se O

Vague Adam:	Dear corpse, says he.
Westwest:	In my regimental small clothes.
Childe scolding a flower:	A vow he made but he kept it very ill.
Flower-de-Luce:	He kept it, perchance, in the conscious shade.
Plank o wude:	I should say you are fond of dark colors and vice-versa.
Westwest:	The contest was hard on both sides.
Flower-de-Luce:	All upon the running corn and all the harm ever I done.
Westwest:	Hithertoo fruitless errands.
Old Sultan:	No, the Prince of Darkness is a gentleman.
Lord Byron:	He looks like a giant hair ball.
20471120:	His boyfriend's an idiot.
Flower-de-Luce:	French Mercury. Frog-bit. Fritillary.
Tragic Mulatto:	Determined to get there first he enters the garden with a private key.
Westwest:	To subordinate the idea of Time to that of likeness.
Old Sultan:	Slang for the pink redoubt.
Tragic Mulatto:	Ba, ba, lilli ba.

THE INFINITY OF SMALL
HIDDEN SPRINGS

Flower-de-Luce: I took myself for a widow
or a bachelor I don't know which.

Plank o wude: All the dewsea vile within.

Flower-de-Luce: And I've lost my good-luck pencil.

Old Sultan: Scrape of the dainties.

Flower-de-Luce: I've never been so tired in my whole life.

Upset Kitty: That body of facts and discoveries.

2047110: Thrild upon a pinn.

Plank o wude: O it took upon her cheek, her cheek,
And it took upon her chin.

Vague Adam: Nothing but bonfires.

Flower-de-Luce: And I seemed to ask her from my thoughts.

FUME TERRE

FDL: I came by your door.
LB: It lay in your road.

FDL: Your dog barkit at me.
LB: It is his use & custom.

FDL: There's a straw at your beard.
LB: I wish it had been a thrave.

FDL: The ox is eating at it.
LB: Were the ox in the water.

FDL: And you must barn it in a mouse-holl
        And thrash it into your shoes soll,

        And you must winnow it in the looff
        And also seck it in your glove.

LB: That is all I ask.

FDL: Dog's wheat, double-tooth, duckmeat.

LB: All I ask, the while we.

FDL: For I crave one kiss of your clay-cold lips.

BLOW BOOK

A Pretty Echo
From the Ruin

I am puzzled in a question about hell
and with it a kiss unfolds in the air
years from now, or just now.
The light is backward, okay,

only a puzzle it throws by the wall.
It would not be too late.
I hear small waves on the shingle beach,
midnight all aglimmer.

Things dreamproof and how they stir.
I can see how some would say:
so this is what cursing does
to words and all they survey,

surplus feeding at the neck of a word.
On the hard lips of a doll a single drop,
a rake, if that's the word, wanting nothing
but to hear the tavern talk.

White Dialogues de Mundo

I was now wearing into the sunshine,
an old wide-awake hat
and a straw bonnet of the plum pudding
sort—if that makes any sense.
I put the hat in my pocket.

Thus the same thing of every thing.
Jargonelle, early pear,
the magical "perforated strap"
leant by Aphrodite to be worn talking
trash and get him bridled seen.

My fears grew less by custom
for I have known people who:
    + take hot or cold baths
    + pinch themselves
And all my favorite places have met with misfortune.

In went the arm up to the shoulder
and then came fear upon us
stealing peas in church time
when the owners was safe to boil at the gypsies' fire
who went half shares at our stolen luxury.

Out it's came the world adieu,
it was a moonlight night.
O row me in a pair o sheets,
the never a bit can I eat or drink
my heart's saw full of pine.

Fond of getting bluebells, the selfsame golden
eye and surfeit with its blushing stains
underneath, under water on May eve. Firstness
tossing pinwheels and cowslip balls
over the garland hung from chimney to chimney.

Breathing flutes, beechen bowls—
I felt the warning for once.
A sizeable gudgeon twinkled round the glossy pebbles.
I'm afraid that's it. Or something afloat on the chance
he won't. Sorrow there was

made fair. Desiderata
One pair of Candlesticks
One better set of China
Two tubs & a pail—a counterpane
A pipe six blankets.

O word's gone to the gamekeeper and his man.
A distinct breezelet of fear. Tea things.
Lov'd the same love & hated the same hate.
Riddle me this. A meadow with now
and then a single arch crossing the meadow.

Hurry Up Moonlight

Chimes at midnight,
windows fly open in thistle-blue cars,
a kingdom of glances tipped to the ground.

Last-minute instructions to love
sail under foot, the man selling
crackers and fruit on the quai

pulls back from the train.
Now all is haste,
kissing with happy cries.

THIEF IN THE CANDLE

Only now, the candles you favored
to summon a mood surprise our limbs,
like the final turn of a parable,
binding the charm of the naked dark.

Look, how summer, flagrant, follows
autumn into yesterday, like a village
forced into hiding, or a man who pays
so much to sleep through seasons

of arias, so that it all takes place in a place
stifled by a dream. Or shall we stop
at nothing? Better to stay and wonder,
I think, to thread this lost smile

like stragglers at Versailles drafted
into a maze. Let lions sleep and rumor
blaze around us. It is too early to speak,
the name withheld shall perish in the open.

Morbidezza

The massive doors stand open:
snow is falling through the chandeliers,
books tumble from their places
until the shelves are bare.

January drifts indoors,
cowling the cook, the soldier, the derelict.
Tiny lamps scallop the aisles,
a tree floods the apron.

The last grains heal the corners,
the ticking. Who kneels to brush
the powder from your face,
the mouth first.

Snow darkens the air again,
falling through my hands
and the dreamproof skiff
your eyes follow.

FAIRY CHASM

Pale looks have many friends.
In the habit of shoulder blades
in the tall grass.
A veritable gold mine of.

We quarrel in secret.
One of us burns to the ground
and then another—it takes hours
to waste its sweetness on the desert air
and hours before your body consents
to be touched, or touched again,
and so coaxed
to knife the pilot,
to queer the flight,
to use the blade for cutting shade
and little last beds.

A mouse crawls into a hive for warmth
one winter: bees prick the intruder
a thousand times, not knowing
when to halt the affair,
but to embalm the rare December guest:
gold leviathan cured by Old Believers
in red dawn jelly.
And the comb climbs
the gods' disabled sable ship,
drones madly building nurseries
over the monster's tomb
—oh curiosity, derelict—
dragging one gorgeous queen
from cell to cell,
legs gone—ground off!
So much the better.

Dead Fairy

The trillium pivots
out of sight—handblown, it says—
swaying against itself, mouth
    to furtive mouth.

Do not ask which half
falls prey, if it appears from nowhere,
fishing at twilight, a face submerged
    and trailing silver

    bubbles. Sweet breath,
unquiet ember clutching April shoots
in shallow water, nest of the unforeseen
    hatching from the stream.

PEARL AND PEARLENE
AT THE AIRPORT

Their horse bodies are poison-proof.

If I began a poem of Spinoza, thus it should begin.

One of which, the common blue flag,
is sometimes called the poison-flag.

In sewing time
partridges towering.

Boys of ten learnt the art
of poisoning their fathers.

A bright ruffledness.

I sat near one of 'em . . . and was almost
Poison'd with a pair of Suede Gloves he wears.

He's liker a woman than a young lord's serving man.

Having stooped to the trade of secret poisoner . . .

She's clade hersell in page array.

According to the quality of the poison-flour it yields.

Gold-headed cane on a pikteresk Toor.

Imprisoned with the poison-bowl
hourly before my eyes.

We still call Bess a maid—from this that
a fallen angel still an angel is.

It wear a sin to kill a sleeping man.

Stone fence, run trembling in a circle.

Peer-Jemmy was puzzen'd they say
by a neighbor who's a witch.

Wept out his eyes of pearl & swom blind after.

The unhairing in the lime-pits is done.

Braille. And the thing took hold.

A poison-ring of curious construction.

The man with one coat.
Does it rain? No—give me
my blue coat then.
Does it rain? Yes! Give me
my blue coat.

To poison his prayer book and a pair of beads.

Things find fames. Man as he is not
by light of that shapely white Cloud,
the day-moon.

The tooth itself crescentic
whose touch is mortal.

Taffeta Punk

Each morning I walk into the woods
to free the orphans and volunteers
collecting in the barn of my mouth.
I stop to say hello to the charcoaler
who never leaves the woods.
His daughter slumbers in a clearing,
blouse and skirt
crumpled beside her.
I blink,
the dwarf owl is a pinecone.
Lamplight of vanilla
born in a wolf's lair.
She stirs in her sleep
—golden grasses
to a pumpkin's sob—
crossing a sea of guests
to the morning of the pupil's blue life.

Whispered Goods

My body came into the hands of an heir,
all at once. There was no other way.
A tree inherits its crown, its thirst,
its signals, and he inherited me.
That makes him a girl
with lakes whole lakes of limbs
to do my bidding. I made him a birdhouse
and he took me to Paris for the season.

He asked me to cut his hair
one day. A mirror he brought
for we had none
and set a chair behind the smokehouse.
I caught myself in the glass
and fought off a dream: two dragonflies
skating the lip of a pond, so close
they could be light threshed from the eaves,
apart from the dither of wasps
about their nests, almost napping
in love. Did I say
he asked me to cut his hair outdoors?
Near the spot where Old Alice died
and a tree came out of her grave,
felled for wood to build the new kitchen.

The New World, he says, is a world
of logical fata morganas.
And these parts are notorious
it's true: ships and barns mount the air.
But he was thinking of his writing machine.
Not to mention the French remedies
for his stomach and French ideas.

When he dies, every hand shall be sold
to cover his debts, the latest being
the sum to build
a chamber clinging like a nest
to the ceiling of the library:
three ports in its façade,
each blank as a mirror.
There may be creatures, sir, who visit there,
but I have never seen their faces
in the foundry or the smokehouse
on Mulberry Row.

NATIVE SPRING

No one sober under the bright canopy,
no one glancing off the street at dusk
sees the angel groom the blaze.
Hundreds of men at tables—
soldiers, farmers in town for a drink,
the mayor himself drunk as a wheelbarrow.
Forearms and boots whitened with flour,
a gauze-capped baker grumbles in his cups.
None sees the angel catch his sleeve
on the grill, stripped as he gathers
the birds from the fire.

Beekeeper Cove

Cicadas roar past noon
to drive a dainty disappearance—sooner godlike
and not to be blinder—into the sea.
A beekeeper, veiled and gloved,
goes silently amidst the hives.

No branch breaks the sun,
wind blows through a ragged fence.
From here, my pocket Pompei,
tricked by starlight and passing ships,
I see you swimming far below.
Dark beds of kelp and lighter stone
glow beneath you in the water,
the faint sound of your splash
rising from the sea.

I am lost—though I can still see you
and the cove where we will meet.
The path divides before it disappears,
before the madrone looms into a mazy reef.
Your movement starlike, unalarmed,
captured now by gulls and silver scales,
tells land from sea.

Black Genoa

Chain plunging through the pipe
like a gale in the trees.
I cleared a patch on the salt-crazed glass
and rose through my eyes
to the rim of a desolate port:
no trace of cattle or tilled fields,
a town glittering like a vein
in the cliff,
livid smoke marbling
the country behind the coast.
Lives abandoned, shop doors agape,
roasts and kettles
still steaming over fires.
A trail of paint
veers from the barber's window,
the brush dropped in the street.

REFRAIN

You didn't say a word at dinner.
Now, asleep beside me,
you're back at the table
playing all the roles but one
in the same drowned voice,
the evening cut to seven minutes:
we all squeeze into the galley
once more, only this time
we speak, if we speak at all,
in a strange tongue. Everyone is happy.
The lobster goes fast, someone spots
the pepper mill across the table
—you reach over me, mumbling, chewing—
I shrink away from your arm.
The underworld of the table
stammers, once, like a boiler
building a head of steam.
Invisible hands
cup the light in your face.
A smoke of a rain sweeps the bay.

DRUMHEAD COURT

Word slips
from hand to hand,
bow to stern: *Idle the engine.*
The bay wakes over the hull.
Dusk to cordial dusk.
The lantern bows its head,
we sail into a drowsy hive.

Starry ides. One door
opens: to the doorman say
Rags for straw.
A ship carved from memory.
You cast up lodging, tapers,
dung mixed with snow.
A ziggurat of foolscap.

The air is cool and turbulent—
something wonderful is burning.
Oh, look how dark
the inlet grows:
your share is gone—
a filthy catch
turns up in your mouth. Say it.

Quartet

Not a parade,
the *triste* in the front seat of the Impala
careening down a side street.
Already forgotten two shots
fired into the teller's face.
Sees but can't be seen,
under the rubric
pneumatica.
Fairest f-stop,
bozo listing
under sunstruck glass.
Two others—a tramp with blue hair
and the driver in a bear suit—
crane their heads out windows
to roar at drunks on the pavement.

And all by himself,
the one they call mother,
his words a hissing tide.

Where have you been sisters,
killing swine?

STOLEN CAR

A lady begs
a soldier for something.

The day is over for the day.

A little fat sigh, I see,
under the downy flake of death.

A glass of cold punch is moving.

Birds sing and fly
through the kissing teens.
And sing.

The sky leads to an untouched forest
untouched by humans anyway
a deer pops out
the hunter fires.
Out of bullets.

Spring is when the dove watches
you fix your duchess.

THE NEW PORNOGRAPHY

At the barn-well thrashing,
at the far well washing

gloves of green and feathers blue
a robe so jimp he sang a grave.

Madhouse &—a stratagem—charming ferry.
The nearest names are still oblivions.

Appearing in a fine egg of light,
clothes & title. Laws upon wrecks.

Think of any card in the pack—
I'll show you the card and the flood.

Northernmost losing its name,
its waters into stranger streams.

What drives their kind, can Willy say,
to make outspeckle o' me?

And he has paid the rescue shot,
has he, with gaud and white monnaie.

Dumb Waiter—Bed—Little Tommy—Cerberus.
Leaves already scattered on the walk.

Think any number you like—double it—
add 12 to it—halve it—

take away the original number
and there remains six.

Judge absent things by the absent:
a gentleman's home sweetly buried.

Sea-shell for the handle of a bell,
cold water for shaving.

A trembling lane of moonlight on the sea,
epaulettes dangling from an Orange Tree.

T'is pitten my head in sick a stir
that flower gains for me.

A Book on Comets The Art of Gauging
The Female Shipwright Hymns Tricks of

London Laid Open Angler Kings. Of church bells
ringing in the middle of the night.

The rime fell thick and we was covered
white as a sheet when we got up.

Program

John Clare. *The Natural History Prose Writings of John Clare*, ed. Margaret Grainger. Oxford: Clarendon Press, 1983.

Samuel Coleridge. *The Notebooks of Samuel Taylor Coleridge*, 8 volumes, eds. Kathleen Coburn and Merton Christensen. Princeton: Bollingen Press, 1957–1990.

Paula Danziger. *Amber Brown Is Not a Crayon*. Scholastic Publishers, 1995.

Catherine de Zegher, ed. *The Prinzhorn Collection: Traces Upon the Wunderblock*. New York: The Drawing Center, 2000.

John S. Farmer, ed. *Musa Pedestris: Three Centuries of Canting Songs and Slang Rhymes*. London, 1896.

Blues lyrics of Blind Willie Johnson.

92

Special thanks
to Molly Bendall
who loaned me a thread in the maze

ABOUT THE AUTHOR

Daniel Tiffany received his training in the theater at the Juilliard
School in New York City. He holds a PhD in Comparative Lit-
erature from the University of Chicago and has published trans-
lations of works by Sophocles, Georges Bataille, and the Italian
poet, Cesare Pavese. His critical works include *Radio Corpse:
Imagism and the Cryptaesthetic of Ezra Pound* (Harvard Univer-
sity Press, 1995) and *Toy Medium: Materialism and Modern Lyric*
(University of California Press, 2000), the latter named one of the
"Best Books of 2000" by the *Los Angeles Times* Book Review. His
poetry has appeared in many journals, including *Tin House, Bos-
ton Review,* and the *Paris Review.* He has held residencies at the
MacDowell Colony and the Karolyi Foundation in France and
been the recipient of a Whiting Fellowship. He lives in Venice,
California and teaches at the University of Southern California.

FREE VERSE EDITIONS

Edited by Jon Thompson

2006

Physis by Nicolas Pesque, translated by Cole Swensen
Puppet Wardrobe by Daniel Tiffany
These Beautiful Limits by Thomas Lisk
The Wash by Adam Clay

2005

A Map of Faring by Peter Riley
Signs Following by Ger Killeen
Winter Journey [*Viaggio d'inverno*] by Attilio Bertolucci, translated by Nicholas Benson

www.ingramcontent.com/pod-product-compliance
Lightning Source LLC
Chambersburg PA
CBHW032018090426

42741CB00006B/653